Kunal Chakraborty
Palash De
Indranil Roy

INDUSTRIAL APPLICATIONS OF PROGRAMMABLE LOGIC CONTROLLERS AND SCADA

Anchor Academic
Publishing

Chakraborty, Kunal, De, Palash, Roy, Indranil: INDUSTRIAL APPLICATIONS OF PROGRAMMABLE LOGIC CONTROLLERS AND SCADA, Hamburg, Anchor Academic Publishing 2016

Buch-ISBN: 978-3-96067-024-7
PDF-eBook-ISBN: 978-3-96067-524-2
Druck/Herstellung: Anchor Academic Publishing, Hamburg, 2016

Bibliografische Information der Deutschen Nationalbibliothek:
Die Deutsche Nationalbibliothek verzeichnet diese Publikation in der Deutschen Nationalbibliografie; detaillierte bibliografische Daten sind im Internet über http://dnb.d-nb.de abrufbar.

Bibliographical Information of the German National Library:
The German National Library lists this publication in the German National Bibliography. Detailed bibliographic data can be found at: http://dnb.d-nb.de

© Anchor Academic Publishing, Imprint der Diplomica Verlag GmbH
Hermannstal 119k, 22119 Hamburg
http://www.diplomica-verlag.de, Hamburg 2016
Printed in Germany

ABSTRACT

Abstract: The book contains various applications of programmable logic controllers and SCADA designing of a plant. Everyone knows, nowadays every human handled plants are being replaced by the automatic control system, thus called Automation. For the ease of access and for better precision the PLCs are accepted worldwide. In this book Rockwell PLCs are described and so the SCADA design also done by the RSView32 software, manufactured by Rockwell. It is one of the biggest name in the PLC software industry, being easy to use, control and modify. Some electrical drives, such as D.C drives, A.C drives are also described in detail because the control part is done by the PLCs but the main plant is based on these electrical drives.

ACKNOWLEDGEMENTS

We would like to give our sincere gratitude towards Mr. Bablu Bhattacharya, Chairman, IMPS College of Engineering And Technology, Dr. S.K. Bhattacharya, Principal, IMPS College Of Engineering And Technology and Mr. Sankha Subhra Ghosh, H.O.D., Dept. Of Electrical Engineering, IMPSCET for their valuable suggestion and guidance. Without their kind help this book would not have been formed. They gave us their valuable time and information which has helped us to make this book more better.

PREFACE

We have tried to write this book with our every possible positive effort. Various informations and diagrams are given to help the readers to understand the chapter with more ease. This is our initial try of writing, errors may be found in the book. Feedback from the readers is highly appreciated.

TABLE OF CONTENTS

LIST OF FIGURES

CHAPTER 1: INTRODUCTION

It is needless to say that water, a compound of Hydrogen and Oxygen is a valuable natural gift which is very essential for survival of mankind including animals. The water used for portable purposes should be free from undesirable impurities. The water available from untreated sources like Well, Boreholes and Spring is generally not hygienic and safe for drinking. Thus it is desirable and necessary to purify the water and supply under hygienic conditions for human drinking purpose.

In recent times the need of packaged beverages, such as drinking water is very much high. In a beverage packaging industry the purity of the water is given the main priority.

In a beverage industry, there are various steps to manufacture a product.

The materials are stored at various locations in the plant. These materials are to be carefully routed between different points of the plant equipment as a part of beverage manufacturing process. They are required to flow through different pipes depending on the process. All the fixed pipes in a plant for material routing have valves at the intersection points of pipes. To set a path through these pipes for a material flow between any two points, respective valves in the path should be operated in desired manner, depending on the kind of process employed at that point of time.

In today's era mankind are trying to implement some technology, which will decrease its labour. Various technologies are implemented in this aspect, one of them is industrial automation. The automation technology has changed the view of controlling technology. It has made the manufacturing, packaging and various stages of an industry very much precise and human friendly.

CHAPTER 2: WHAT IS PLC?

<u>Definition:-</u>A digitally operating electronic apparatus which uses a programming memory for the internal storage of instructions for implementing specific functions such as logic, sequencing, timing, counting and arithmetic to control through digital or analog modules, various types of machines or process.

<u>Historical background:</u> The controller had to be designed in modular form, so that sub-assemblies could be removed easily for replacement or repair.

The control system needed the capability to pass data collection to a central system. The system had to be reusable. The method used to program the controller had to be simple, so that it could be easily understood by plant personnel.

Some years of implementation of PLC devices is mentioned below:

<u>1968:</u> Programmable concept developed

<u>1969:</u> Hardware CPU controller, with logic instructions, 1 K of memory and 128 I/O points

<u>1974:</u> Use of several (multi) processors within a PLC - timers and counters; arithmetic operations; 12 K of memory and 1024 I/O points

<u>1976:</u> Remote input/output systems introduced

<u>1977:</u> Microprocessors - based PLC introduced

<u>1980</u> :Intelligent I/O modules developed (Enhanced communications facilities, Enhanced software features)e.g. documentation

   • Use of personal microcomputers as programming aids

<u>1983</u>: Low - cost small PLC's introduced

<u>1985 :</u> Networking of all levels of PLC, computer and machine using SCADA software.

Some PLC Renowned Manufacturers Are:

1. Allen Bradley
2. Gould Modicon
3. Texas Instruments
4. General Electric

5. Westinghouse

6. Cutter Hammer

7. Square D

8. Siemens

9. Klockner & Mouller

10. Festo

11. Telemechanique

12. Toshiba

13. Omron

14. Fanuc

15. Mitsubishi

Application Fields Of PLC:

◎ Manufacturing / Machining

◎ Food / Beverage

◎ Metals

◎ Power

◎ Mining

◎ Petrochemical / Chemical

PLC Size:

1. SMALL - it covers units with up to 128 I/O's and

memories up to 2 Kbytes, these PLC's are capable of providing simple to advance levels or machine controls.

2. MEDIUM- have up to 2048 I/O's and memories up to 32 Kbytes.

3. LARGE - the most sophisticated units of the PLC family. They have up to 8192 I/O's and memories up to 750 Kbytes.

- can control individual production   processes or entire plant.

Control engineering has evolved over time. In the past humans were the main methods for controlling a system. More recently electricity has been used for control and early electrical control based on relays. These relays allow power to be switched on and off without a mechanical switch.It is common to use relays to make simple logical control decisions. The development of low cost computer has brought the most recent revolution, the Programmable Logic Controller (PLC) . The advent of the PLC began in the 1970s, and has become the most common choice for manufacturing controls. PLCs have been gaining popularity on the factory floor and will probably remain predominant for some time to come. Most of this is because of the advantages they offer. Cost effective for controlling complex systems.

• Flexible and can be reapplied to control other systems quickly and easily.

• Computational abilities allow more sophisticated control.

• Trouble shooting aids make programming easier and reduce downtime.

Reliable components make these likely to operate for years before failure. The PLC was invented in response to the needs of the American automotive manufacturing industry. Programmable logic controllers were initially adopted by the automotive industry where software revision replaced the rewiring of hard-wired control panels when production models changed. Before the PLC, control, sequencing, and safety interlock logic for manufacturing automobiles was accomplished using hundreds or thousands of relays, cam timers, and drum sequencers and dedicated closed-loop controllers. The process for updating such facilities for the yearly model change-over was very time consuming and expensive, as electricians needed to individually rewire each and every relay. Digital computers, being general-purpose programmable devices, were soon applied to control of industrial processes. Early computers required specialist programmers, and stringent operating environmental control for temperature, cleanliness, and power quality. Using a general-purpose computer for process control required protecting the computer from the plant floor conditions. An industrial control computer would have several attributes: it would tolerate the shop-floor environment, it would support discrete (bit-form) input and output in an easily extensible manner, it would not require years of training to use, and it would permit its operation to be monitored. The response time of any computer system must be fast enough to be useful for control; the required speed varying according to the nature of the process . In 1968 GM Hydramatic (the automatic transmission division of General Motors) issued a request for proposal for an electronic replacement for hard-wired relay systems. The winning proposal came from Bedford Associates of Bedford, Massachusetts. The first PLC, designated the 084 because it was Bedford Associates' eighty-fourth project, was the result . Bedford Associates started a new company dedicated to developing, manufacturing, selling, and servicing this new product: Modicum, which stood for Modular Digital Controller. One of the people who worked on that project was Dick Morley, who is considered to be the "father" of the PLC. The Modicon brand was sold in 1977 to Gould Electronics, and later acquired by German Company AEG and then by French Schneider Electric, the current owner. One of the very first 084 models built is now on display at Modicon's headquarters in North Andover, Massachusetts. It was presented to Modicon by GM, when the unit was retired after nearly twenty years of uninterrupted service. Modicon used the 84 moniker at the end of its product range until the 984 made its appearance. The automotive industry is still one of the largest users of PLCs.

Early PLCs were designed to replace relay logic systems. These PLCs were programmed in "ladder logic", which strongly resembles a schematic diagram of relay logic. This program notation was chosen to reduce training demands for the existing technicians. Other early PLCs used a form of instruction list programming, based on a stack-based logic solver. Modern PLCs can be programmed in a variety of ways.

Programmable logic controllers have been used extensively in industrial control applications since their advent in the 70s. The programming of logic controllers has been done majorly by the knowledge of the programmer and no formal methods are used. Hence, the task of writing the code becomes a difficult one with the efficiency of the code varying from programmer to programmer. The ladder logic structure of coding PLCs makes it difficult to realize higher level concepts such as function calls and looping. The discrete event based modeling of systems provides a suitable sequential structure to the programming of PLCs.

ROLE OF ELECTRONICS IN AUTOMATION

A constant demand for better and more efficient manufacturing and process machinery has led to the requirement for higher quality and reliability in control techniques. With the availability of intelligent, compact solid state electronic devices, it has been possible to provide control systems that can reduce maintenance, down time and improve productivity to a great extend. By installing efficient and user friendly industrial electronics systems for manufacturing machinery or processors, one can obtain a precise, reliable and prolific means for generating quality products.

Considering the varied demand and increasing competition, one has to provide for flexible manufacturing process. One of the latest techniques in solid state controls that offers flexible and efficient operation to the user is "PROGRAMMABLE CONTROLLERS". The basic idea behind these programmable controllers was to provide means to eliminate high cost associated with inflexible, conventional relay controlled systems. Programmable controllers offer a system with computer flexibility:

1. Suited to withstand the industrial environment
2. Has simplicity of operation
3. Maintenance by plant technicians.
4. Reduce machine down time and provide expandability for future.

In recent times, the programmable logic controllers have gone through various stages of development, and have become more and more reliable, time saving device.

Some major components of a PLC is discussed below:

The PLC system

A programmable logic controller consists of the following components:

- Central Processing Unit (CPU)
- Memory
- Input modules
- Output modules
- Power supply.

A PLC hardware block diagram is shown in Figure . The programming terminal in the diagram is not a part of the PLC, but it is essential to have a terminal for programming or monitoring a PLC. In the diagram, the arrows between blocks indicate the information and power flowing directions.

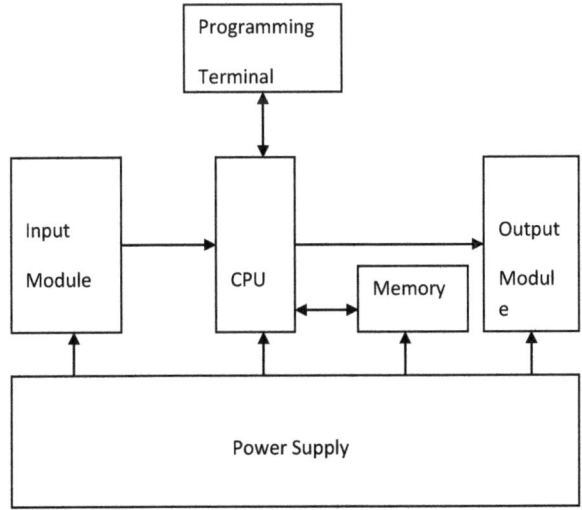

Fig 1.Basic Components Of a PLC

CPU

Like other computerized devices, there is a Central Processing Unit (CPU) in a PLC. The CPU, which is the "brain" of a PLC, does the following operations:

- Updating inputs and outputs. This function allows a PLC to read the status of its input terminals and energize or deenergize its output terminals.
- Performing logic and arithmetic operations. A CPU conducts all the mathematic and logic operations involved in a PLC.
- Communicating with memory. The PLC's programs and data are stored in memory. When a PLC is operating, its CPU may read or change the contents of memory locations.
- Scanning application programs. An application program, which is called a *ladder logic program*, is a set of instructions written by a PLC programmer. The scanning function allows the PLC to execute the application program as specified by the programmer.
- Communicating with a programming terminal. The CPU transfers program and data between itself and the programming terminal.

A PLC's CPU is controlled by operating system software. The operating system software is a group of supervisory programs that are loaded and stored permanently in the PLC's memory by the PLC manufacturer.

Memory

Memory is the component that stores information, programs, and data in a PLC. The process of putting new information into a memory location is called *writing*. The process of retrieving information from a memory location is called *reading*.

The common types of memory used in PLCs are Read Only Memory (ROM) and Random Access Memory (RAM). A ROM location can be read, but not written. ROM is used to store programs and data that should not be altered. For example, the PLC's operating programs are stored in ROM.

A RAM location can be read or written. This means the information stored in a RAM location can be retrieved and/or altered. Ladder logic programs are stored in RAM. When a new ladder logic program is loaded into a PLC's memory, the old program that was stored in the same locations is over-written and essentially erased.

The memory capacities of PLCs vary. Memory capacities are often expressed in terms of *kilo-bytes* (K). One byte is a group of 8 bits. One bit is a memory location that may store one binary number that has the value of either 1 or 0. (Binary numbers are addressed in Module 2). 1K memory means that there are 1024 bytes of RAM. 16K memory means there are 16 x 1024 =16384 bytes of RAM.

Input modules and output modules

A PLC is a control device. It takes information from inputs and makes decisions to energize or de-energize outputs. The decisions are made based on the statuses of inputs and outputs and the ladder logic program that is being executed.

The input devices used with a PLC include pushbuttons, limit switches, relay contacts, photo sensors, proximity switches, temperature sensors, and the like. These input devices can be AC (alternating current) or DC (direct current). The input voltages can be high or low. The input signals can be digital or analog. Differing inputs require different input modules. An input module provides an interface between input devices and a PLC's CPU, which uses only a low DC voltage. The input module's function is to convert the input signals to DC voltages that are acceptable to the CPU. Standard discrete input modules include 24 V AC, 48 V AC, 120 V AC, 220 V AC, 24 V DC, 48 V DC, 120 V DC, 220 V DC, and transistor-transistor logic (TTL) level.

The devices controlled by a PLC include relays, alarms, solenoids, fans, lights, and motor starters. These devices may require different levels of AC or DC voltages. Since the signals processed in a PLC are low DC voltages, it is the function of the output module to convert PLC control signals to the voltages required by the controlled circuits or devices. Standard discrete output modules include 24 V AC, 48 V AC, 120 V AC, 220 V AC, 24 V DC, 48 V DC, 120 V DC, 220 V DC, and TTL level.

Different Types OF I/O Modules:

1. Pilot Duty Outputs

Outputs of this type typically are used to drive high-current electromagnetic loads such as solenoids, relays, valves, and motor starters.

These loads are highly inductive and exhibit a large inrush current.

Pilot duty outputs should be capable of withstanding an inrush current of 10 times the rated load for a short period of time without failure.

2. General - Purpose Outputs

These are usually low- voltage and low-current and are used to drive indicating lights and other non-inductive loads. Noise suppression may or may not be included on this types of modules.

3. Discrete Inputs

Circuits of this type are used to sense the status of limit switches, push buttons, and other discrete sensors. Noise suppression is of great importance in preventing false indication of inputs turning on or off because of noise.

4. Analog I/O

Circuits of this type sense or drive analog signals.

Analog inputs come from devices, such as thermocouples, strain gages, or pressure sensors, that provide a signal voltage or current that is derived from the process variable.

Standard Analog Input signals: 4-20mA; 0-10V

Analog outputs can be used to drive devices such as voltmeters, X-Y recorders, servomotor drives, and valves through the use of transducers.

Standard Analog Output signals: 4-20mA; 0-5V; 0-10V

5. Special - Purpose I/O

Circuits of this type are used to interface PLCs to very specific types of circuits such as servomotors, stepping motors PID (proportional plus integral plus derivative) loops, high-speed pulse counting, resolver and decoder inputs, multiplexed displays, and keyboards.

This module allows for limited access to timer and counter presets and other PLC variables without requiring a program loader.

Power Supply

PLCs are powered by standard commercial AC power lines. However, many PLC components, such as the CPU and memory, utilize 5 volts or another level of DC power. The PLC power supply converts AC power into DC power to support those components of the PLC.

Programming Terminal

A PLC requires a programming terminal and programming software for operation. The programming terminal can be a dedicated terminal or a generic computer purchased anywhere. The programming terminal is used for programming the PLC and monitoring the PLC's operation. It may also download a ladder logic program (the sending of a program from the programming terminal to the PLC) or upload a ladder logic program (the sending of a program from the PLC to the programming terminal). The terminal uses programming software for programming and "talking" to a PLC.

Some Major Components Of A PLC:

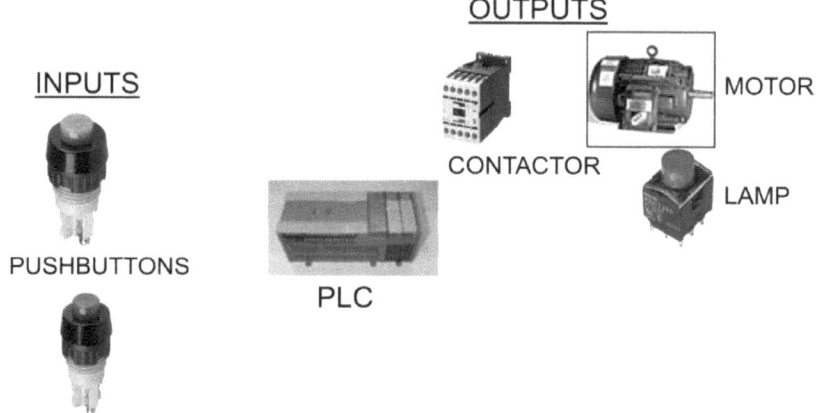

Fig2. Some I/O devices Of PLC

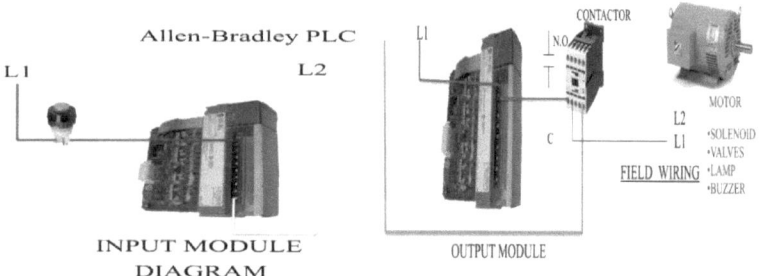

Fig3. I/O Module Of Allen-Bradley PLC

Basic Operations of PLC:

Discrete Inputs:-

A discrete input also referred as digital input is an input that is either ON or OFF are connected to the PLC digital input. In the ON condition it is referred to as logic 1 or a logic high and in the OFF condition maybe referred to as logic o or logic low.

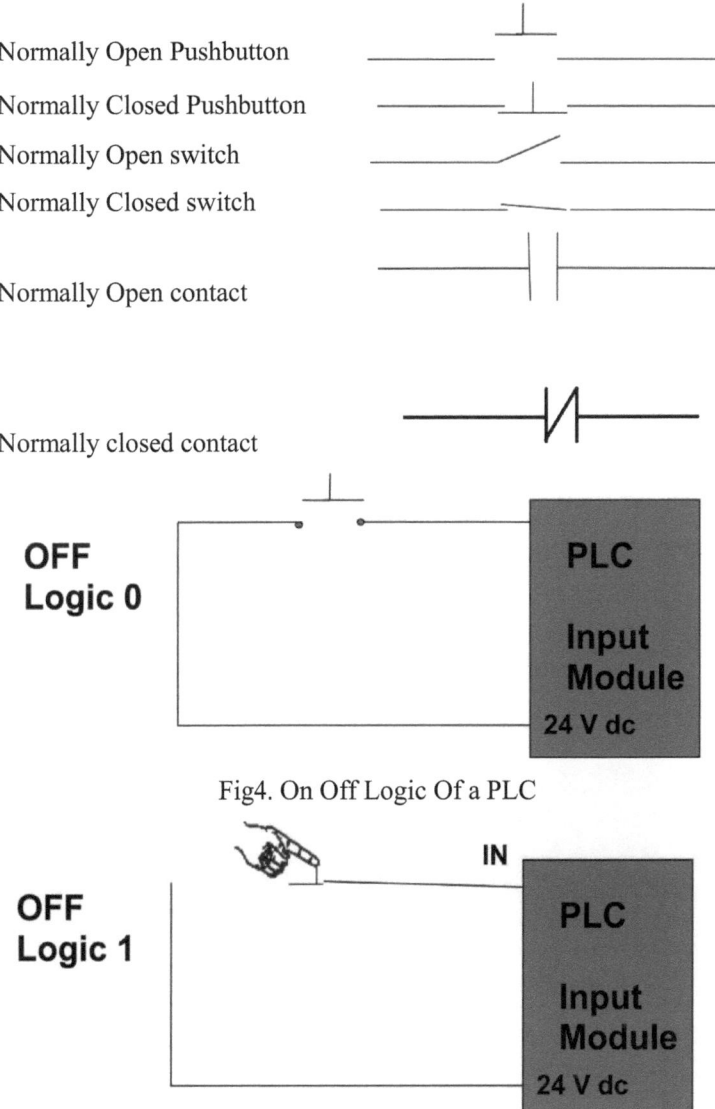

Normally Open Pushbutton

Normally Closed Pushbutton

Normally Open switch

Normally Closed switch

Normally Open contact

Normally closed contact

OFF
Logic 0

Fig4. On Off Logic Of a PLC

OFF
Logic 1

Analog Input:- An analog input is an input signal that has a continuous signal. Typical inputs may vary from 0 to 20mA, 4 to 20Ma or 0 to10V. Below, a level transmitter monitors the level of liquid in the tank. Depending on the level Tank, the signal to the PLC can either increase or decrease as the level increases or decreases.

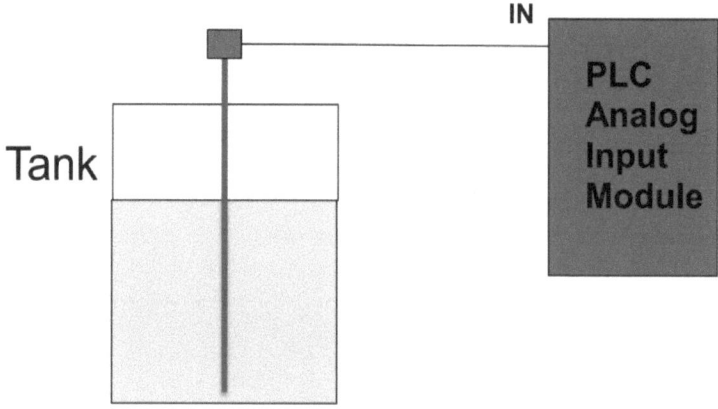

Fig5. Input Logic Of PLC

Digital Output:- A discrete output is either in an ON or OFF condition. Solenoids, contactors coils, lamps are example of devices connected to the Discrete or digital outputs. Below, the lamp can be turned ON or OFF by the PLC output it is connected to.

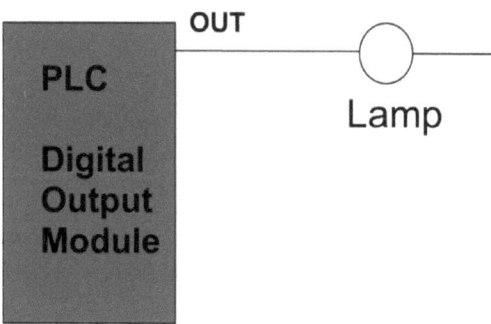

Fig 6. Output Logic Of a PLC

Analog Output:-

An analog output is an output signal that has a continuous signal. Typical outputs may vary from 0 to 20mA, 4 to 20mA or 0 to10V.

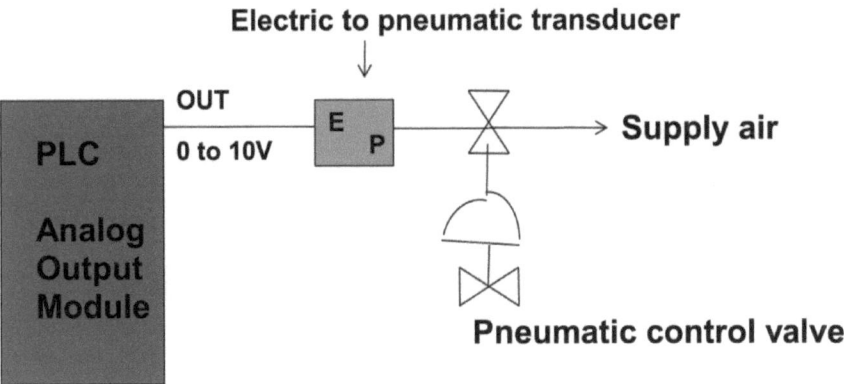

Fig7.Analog Output Of a PLC

Processor:-The processor module contains the PLC's microprocessor, its supporting circuitry, and its memory system. The main function of the microprocessor is to analyze data coming from field sensors through input modules, make decisions based on the user's defined control program and return signal back through output modules to the field devices. Field sensors: switches, flow, level, pressure, temp. transmitters, etc. Field output devices: motors, valves, solenoids, lamps, or audible devices.

The memory system in the processor module has two parts: a system memory and an application memory.

Memory Map Organization

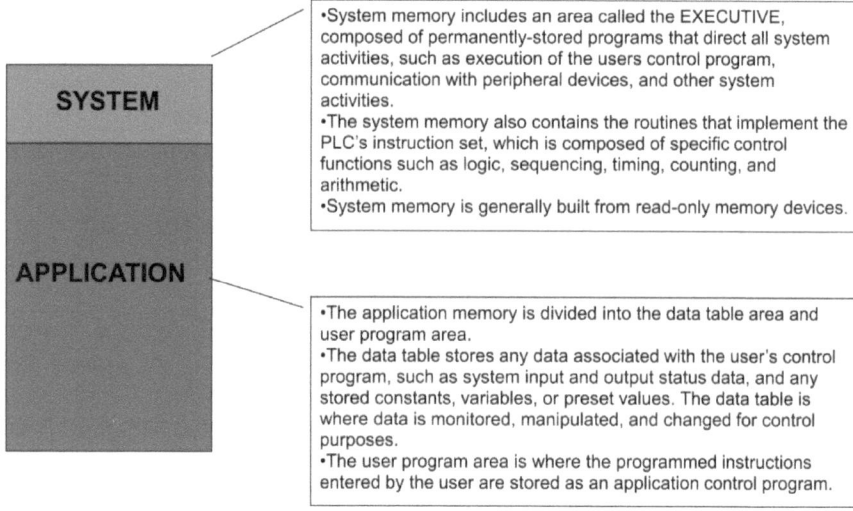

Fig8. Memory Map Organisation

Memory Designs:-

Volatile Memory:-A volatile memory is one that loses its stored information when power is removed.

Even momentary losses of power will erase any information stored or programmed on a volatile memory chip.

Common Type of Volatile Memory:

RAM:- Random Access Memory(Read/Write)

Read/write indicates that the information stored in the memory can be retrieved or read, while write indicates that the user can program or write information into the memory.

The words random access refer to the ability of any location (address) in the memory to be accessed or used. Ram memory is used for both the user memory (ladder diagrams) and storage memory in many PLC's.

RAM memory must have battery backup to retain or protect the stored program.

Several Types of RAM Memory:

1.MOS

2.HMOS

3.CMOS

The CMOS-RAM (Complimentary Metal Oxide Semiconductor) is probably one of the most popular. CMOS-RAM is popular because it has a very low current drain when not being accessed (15microamps.), and the information stored in memory can be retained by as little as 2Vdc.

NON-VOLATILE

Has the ability to retain stored information when power is removed, accidentally or intentionally. These memories do not require battery back-up.

Common Type of Non-Volatile Memory

ROM, Read Only Memory

Read only indicates that the information stored in memory can be read only and cannot be changed. Information in ROM is placed there by the manufacturer for the internal use and operation of the PLC.

Other Types of Non-Volatile Memory

PROM, Programmable Read Only Memory.

Allows initial and/or additional information to be written into the chip.

PROM may be written into only once after being received from the PLC manufacturer; programming is accomplish by pulses of current.

The current melts the fusible links in the device, preventing it from being reprogrammed. This type of memory is used to prevent unauthorized program changes.

EPROM, Erasable Programmable Read Only Memory

Ideally suited when program storage is to be semi-permanent or additional security is needed to prevent unauthorized program changes.

The EPROM chip has a quartz window over a silicon material that contains the electronic integrated circuits. This window normally is covered by an opaque material, but when the opaque material is removed and the circuitry exposed to ultra violet light, the memory content can be erased.

The EPROM chip is also referred to as UVPROM.

EEPROM, Electrically Erasable Programmable Read Only Memory

Also referred to as E^2PROM, is a chip that can be programmed using a standard programming device and can be erased by the proper signal being applied to the erase pin.

EEPROM is used primarily as a non-volatile backup for the normal RAM memory. If the program in RAM is lost or erased, a copy of the program stored on an EEPROM chip can be down loaded into the RAM.

Basic Function of a Typical PLC :-

Read all field input devices via the input interfaces, execute the user program stored in application memory, then, based on whatever control scheme has been programmed by the user, turn the field output devices on or off, or perform whatever control is necessary for the process application.

This process of sequentially reading the inputs, executing the program in memory, and updating the outputs is known as scanning.

While the PLC is running, the scanning process includes the following four phases, which are repeated continuously as individual cycles of operation:

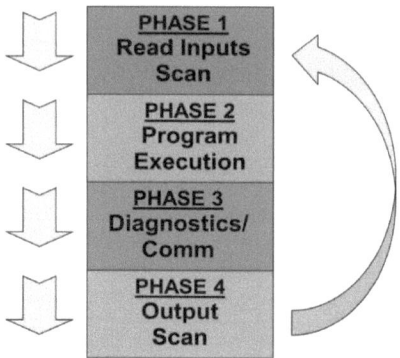

Fig9. PLC Scan Cycle

A PLC scan cycle begins with the CPU reading the status of its inputs.

PHASE 2– Logic Solve/Program Execution

The application program is executed using the status of the inputs

PHASE 3– Logic Solve/Program Execution

Once the program is executed, the CPU performs diagnostics and communication tasks.

An output status scan is then performed, whereby the stored output values are sent to actuators and other field output devices. The cycle ends by updating the outputs.

PHASE 4 - Output Status Scan

As soon as Phase 4 are completed, the entire cycle begins again with Phase 1 input scan.

The time it takes to implement a scan cycle is called SCAN TIME. The scan time composed of the program scan time, which is the time required for solving the control program, and the I/O update time, or time required to read inputs and update outputs. The program scan time generally depends on the amount of memory taken by the control program and type of instructions used in the program. The time to make a single scan can vary from 1 ms to 100 ms.

Common Uses of PLC Communications Ports

◎ Changing resident PLC programs - uploading/downloading from a supervisory controller (Laptop or desktop computer).

◎ Forcing I/O points and memory elements from a remote terminal.

◎ Linking a PLC into a control hierarchy containing several sizes of PLC and computer.

◎ Monitoring data and alarms, etc. via printers or Operator Interface Units (OIUs).

Serial Communications

PLC communications facilities normally provides serial transmission of information.

Common Standards

RS 232

◎ Used in short-distance computer communications, with the majority of computer hardware and peripherals.

◎ Has a maximum effective distance of approx. 30 m at 9600 baud.

Local Area Network (LAN)

Local Area Network provides a physical link between all devices plus providing overall data exchange management or protocol, ensuring that each device can "talk" to other machines and understand data received from them.

LANs provide the common, high-speed data communications bus which interconnects any or all devices within the local area.

LANs are commonly used in business applications to allow several users to share costly software packages and peripheral equipment such as printers and hard disk storage.

RS 422 / RS 485

◎ Used for longer-distance links, often between several PCs in a distributed system. RS 485 can have a maximum distance of about 1000 meters.

Programmable Controllers and Networks

Manufacturer	Network
Allen–Bradley	Data Highway
Gould Modicon	Modbus
General Electric	GE Net Factory LAN
Mitsubishi	Melsec-NET
Square D	SY/NET
Texas Instruments	TIWAY

Fig 10.Dedicated Network System of Different Manufacturers

Specifications:

Several factors are used for evaluating the quality and performance of programmable controllers when selecting a unit for a particular application. These are listed below.

NUMBER OF I /O PORTS

This specifies the number of I/O devices that can be connected to the controller. There should be sufficient I/O ports to meet present requirements with enough spares to provide for moderate future expansion.

Selecting a PLC:

Criteria

•Number of logical inputs and outputs.

•Memory

•Number of special I/O modules

•Scan Time

•Communications

•Software

Detailed Design of a PLC:

1. Understand the process

2. Hardware/software selection

3. Develop ladder logic

4. Determine scan times and memory requirements.

OUTPUT-PORT POWER RATINGS

Each output port should be capable of supplying sufficient voltage and current to drive the output peripheral connected to it.

SCAN TIME

This is the speed at which the controller executes the relay-ladder logic program. This variable is usually specified as the scan time per 1000 logic nodes and typically ranges from 1 to 200 milliseconds.

MEMORY CAPACITY

The amount of memory required for a particular application is related to the length of the program and the complexity of the control system. Simple applications having just a few relays do not require significant amount of memory. Program length tend to expand after the system have been used for a while. It is advantageous to a acquire a controller that has more memory than is presently needed.

PLC Status Indicators

- Power On
- Run Mode
- Programming Mode
- Fault

Troubleshooting

- Look at the process

- PLC status lights

- HALT - something has stopped the CPU

- RUN - the PLC thinks it is OK (and probably is)

- ERROR - a physical problem has occurred with the PLC

- Indicator lights on I/O cards and sensors

- Consult the manuals, or use software if available.

- Use programming terminal / laptop.

List of items required when working with PLCs:

- Programming Terminal - laptop or desktop PC.

- PLC Software. PLC manufacturers have their own specific software and license key.

- Communication cable for connection from Laptop to PLC.

- Backup copy of the ladder program (on diskette, CDROM, hard disk, flash memory). If none, upload it from the PLC.

- Documentation- (PLC manual, Software manual, drawings, ladder program printout, and Seq. of Operations manual.)

Examples of PLC Programming Software:

1. Allen-Bradley – Rockwell Software RSLogix500

2. Modicon - Modsoft

3. Omron - Syswin

4. GE-Fanuc Series 6 – LogicMaster6

5. Square D- PowerLogic

6. Texas Instruments – Simatic

6. Telemecanique – Modicon TSX Micro

PROGRAMMING:

Normally Open
(NO)

Normally Closed
(NC)

Fig 11.NO Contact

Fig 12.NC Contact

Power flows through these contacts when they are closed. The normally open (NO) is true when the input or output status bit controlling the contact is 1. The normally closed (NC) is true when the input or output status bit controlling the contact is 0.

Coils

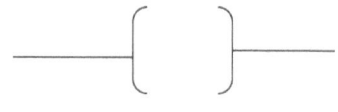

Fig 13.Coils

Coils represent relays that are energized when power flows to them. When a coil is energized it causes a corresponding output to turn on by changing the state of the status bit controlling the output to 1. That same output status bit maybe used to control normally open or normally closed contact anywhere in the program.

Boxes

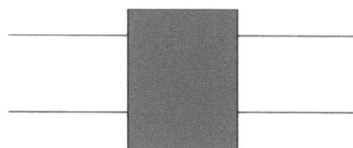

Fig14. Boxes

Boxes represent various instructions or functions that are Executed when power flows to the box. Some of these Functions are timers, counters and math operations.

AND OPERATION

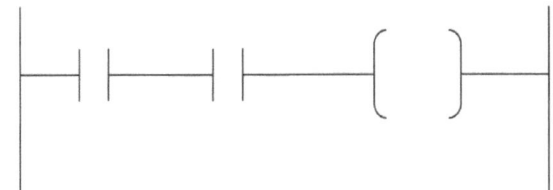

Fig 15.AND Operation Rung

OR OPERATION

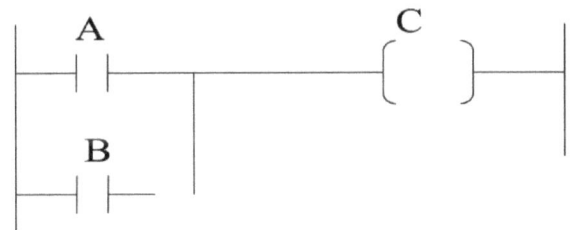

Fig 16.OR Operation Rung

In the rung above, it can be seen that either input A or B is be true (1), or both are true, then the output C is true (1).

NOT OPERATION

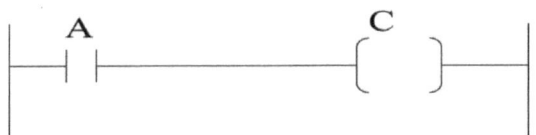

Fig 17.NOT Operation Rung

In the rung above, it can

be seen that if input A is be true (1), then the output C is true (0) or when A is (0), output C is 1.

LADDER LOGIC

There are various methods of programming a PLC. Two of these include Ladder Logic and Function Block Diagrams. The choice of which method is dependent on whether the operation being automated is machine control or process control oriented. Ladder Logic is the method of choice in the case of machine control and Function Block for process control.

Ladder Schematics

Electricians are familiar and comfortable with ladder schematics. These diagrams depict two vertical lines called rails. The rails provide power to the circuitry of the schematic. The power can be AC or DC and the voltage may vary depending on the requirements. Standard labeling for rails is L1 and L2.

Circuitry is placed between the rails connecting the two power lines. These individual lines are referred to as rungs. The circuitry is typically very specific for ladder schematics. For instance, in the following diagram note the first rung consists of a start button that is actually a momentary switch.

Ladder Rung

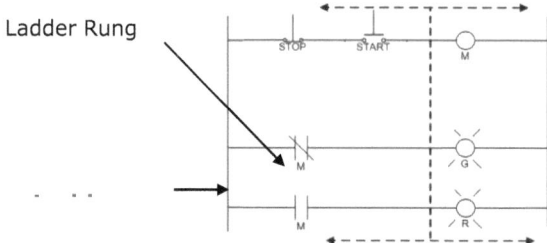

Fig 18.Ladder Logic

Rungs are composed of inputs and outputs. If an imaginary line is drawn down the middle of the previous diagram all the inputs (switches, etc.) are located to the left. Outputs (lights, etc.) are located to the right. Locating all inputs on the left side of a rung and all outputs on the right is good design practice but not required. The latest software versions allow inputs and outputs to be intermixed on a single rung.

Ladder Diagrams

Ladder diagrams are very similar to ladder schematics. A ladder diagram is a symbolic representation of an electrical circuit. That is, specifics concerning switches, etc. are replaced with generic symbols but the same functionality is represented. The primary factor driving the ladder logic design was the requirement to make the system as familiar as possible to the primary users: electricians. Therefore, the symbols utilized closely resemble (if not identical to) schematic symbols for electrical devices. The following diagram is the ladder logic equivalent of the previous ladder schematic.

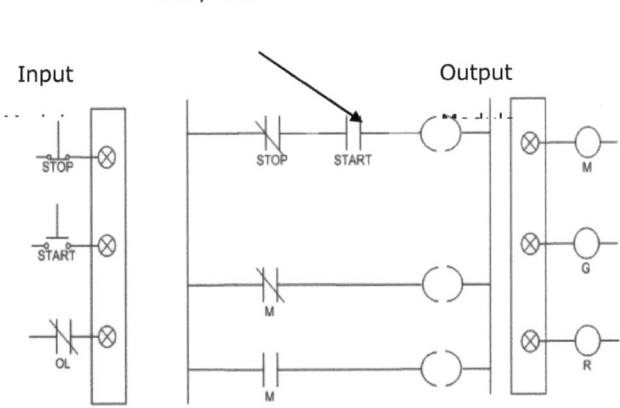

Fig 19.Ladder Diagram with I/O detail included.

Note each device from the ladder schematic has been replaced with an equivalent symbol. The result is a collection of input and output symbols that represent the general operation of the device but not how that action is achieved. Also note that representing a switch or output device generically means the ladder diagram simply represents the function of a switch or motor by whether it is closed/open or off/on, respectively.

Outputs and Inputs/Sensors

Outputs from a PLC are referred to as coils on a ladder diagram. A coil may represent a motor, light, pump, counter, timer, relay, etc. The following displays how a coil is represented in a ladder diagram.

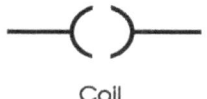

Coil

Fig 20.Coil representation in a ladder diagram.

Inputs/Sensors to a PLC are referred to as Contacts and may consist of switches, buttons, etc. Contacts begin in one of two states normally open or normally closed. A graphical representation of a normally open and closed contact is depicted as it would appear in a ladder diagram.

Normally Open Contact   Normally Closed Contact

Fig 21.Normally Open and Closed representation in a ladder diagram.

These contacts have an initial and follow-on state. The states are best described if the contact is thought of as a switch. Normally open describes a switch whose initial state is open. Therefore, with power applied to both rails of a ladder diagram the initial state of a normally open switch would not complete the connection. When activated the switch changes to its follow-on state. That is, the switch closes completing the connection between the ladder rails. Switch positions for both states are shown in the following Figure.

Initial State

Fig 22.Follow–On State

Fig 23.The NO and NC schematic representation for a limit switch.

Note that simply applying power to the rails will not necessarily result in a follow-on state for a contact.

The DC equivalent circuit and ladder diagram for a normally open contact follows:

Normally Closed describes a switch whose initial state is closed. When activated the switch changes to an open state. The following diagram depicts a normally closed push button and how it will operate when connected to a light and battery. If the button is not pressed then the circuit is complete and the light is on. However, if the button is pressed or activated the circuit is broken and the light is off.

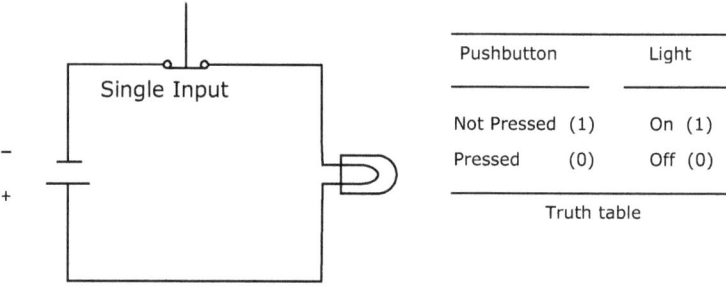

Pushbutton	Light
Not Pressed (1)	On (1)
Pressed (0)	Off (0)

Truth table

Fig 24.Pushbutton Application

Circuit schematic of a NC pushbutton and light and the circuit's truth table. The light will be on (initial state) if the pushbutton is not pressed.

This circuit is represented in a ladder diagram as follows:

If the push button, in the diagram, is a normally open contact then the initial state would be an incomplete circuit and the light will be off. When pressed the button changes states from open to close and the circuit is completed thereby powering the light.

Fundamental Logic

Situations will arise that require two or more events to occur prior to activation of a coil (output device). That is, switch A and switch B must both be closed (or be true) for the light to turn on. The relation between switches A and B and the light is referred to as an 'AND' function. The following depicts a circuit, truth table, and the logical gate for this 'AND' relationship. The truth table shows all the switch position combinations and the resulting outcome for the light. The AND gate is a graphical method for representing AND situations in a logic diagram.

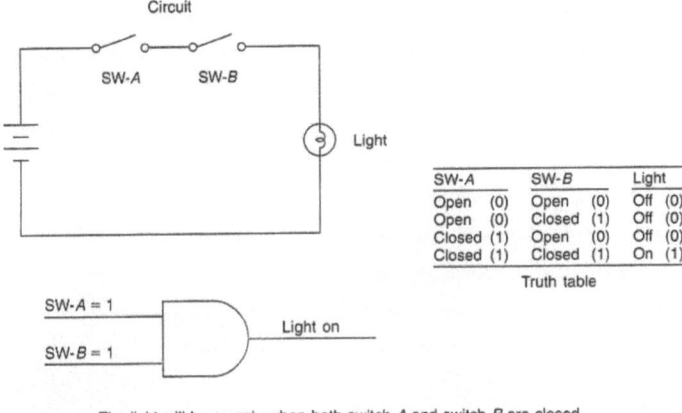

The light will be on only when both switch A and switch B are closed.

Fig 25.Circuit schematic with an AND configuration.

The end result is every contact AND ed together must be closed for the light to activate.

A problem statement depicting an AND situation might be:

A drill press requires the operator to have one hand on each switch before the machine will activate. Switch A and B represent the hand-activated switches and the light turning on simulates the drill press activation.

Launching of nuclear missiles is also an AND scenario. Two keys must be turned simultaneously to launch. What is another AND scenario?

Problem statements will sometimes include situations calling for an output to be triggered by any number of individual or unrelated events. That is, either switch A or B must be closed (or be true) for the light to turn on. The relation between switches A, B and the light is referred to as an 'OR' function. The following depicts a circuit, truth table, and the logical gate for this 'OR' relationship.

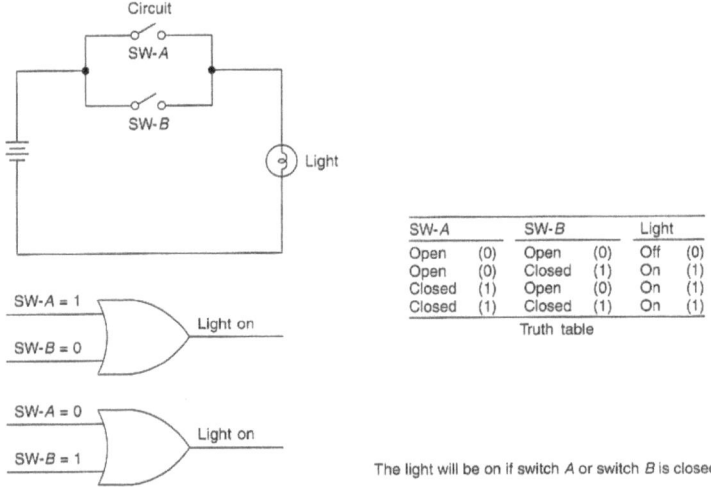

SW-A		SW-B		Light	
Open	(0)	Open	(0)	Off	(0)
Open	(0)	Closed	(1)	On	(1)
Closed	(1)	Open	(0)	On	(1)
Closed	(1)	Closed	(1)	On	(1)

Truth table

The light will be on if switch A or switch B is closed.

Fig 26.Circuit schematic with an OR configuration.

Reviewing the OR truth table indicates the differences between ORs and ANDs. Any of the OR options is sufficient to activate the light by itself or in combination with any of the other or all of the OR options. When depicting OR scenarios in ladder diagrams each option is referred to as a branch.

The corresponding ladder diagram for the previous OR scenario is:

A problem statement depicting the OR situation might be:

Stopping a garage door in an emergency situation may be accomplished by either pressing the stop button or by placing an object in the path of the electric eye. Switch A represents the stop button, switch B represents the electric eye sensor and the light represents the garage door. If the light is on the garage door is stopped.

What are some other OR scenarios?

Ladder Diagram Rules

1. A ladder diagram is read like a book; from left to right and from top to bottom

2. The vertical power lines or rails may be labeled L1, L2 or they may be labeled X1, X2 when the voltage potential is derived from a transformer

3. Devices or components are shown in order of importance whenever possible. Stop buttons should be given a higher order of importance and therefore be shown ahead of other devices.

4. Electrical devices are shown in their normal condition. The normal condition of electrical diagrams is the circuit de-energized and with no external forces such as pressure, flow, etc. acting on the device.

5. Contacts associated with relays, timers, motor starters, etc. always have the same number or letter designation as the device that controls them. This holds true no matter where the contacts appear in the circuit. For example, in the ladder diagram presented on page 15, note the coil labeled M on rung 1. Then note the two contacts in rungs 2 and 3 both have an M below them. This signifies these contacts as being controlled by the coil in rung 1.

6. All contacts associated with a device change state when the device is energized. In regard to the previous example when the coil in rung 1 is activated then any contact controlled by that coil will change from its current state to the follow-on state. Therefore, in rung 2 the Normally Closed (NC) contact will open. The Normally Open (NO) contact in rung 3 will close.

7. Devices that perform a STOP function are normally placed in series on a rung.

8. Devices that perform a START function are normally placed in parallel or in a branch configuration.

Branch Instructions

There are often occasions when it is desired to turn on an output for more than one condition. For example, the doorbell should sound if either the front or rear door button is pushed. The OR option created by the front or rear door button activating the bell is produced in ladder diagrams through a branch. The branch produces two paths that may activate the doorbell.

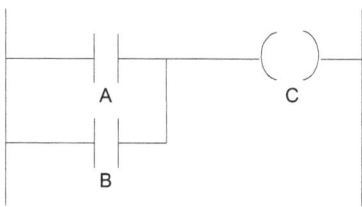

Fig 27.An Or branch for front and rear door bell operation.

If the front door switch (A) is closed, electricity can flow to the bell. Or if the rear door switch (B) is closed, electricity can flow through the bottom branch to the bell. That is, if at least one of the parallel branches forms a true logic path, the run logic is enabled.

Branches may be composed of single or multiple components. Note in the following the first branch consists of an AND function and the lower branch is simply a single component.

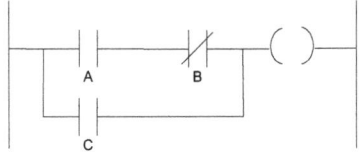

Fig 28.A compound branch configuration.

Coil D is activated when either A and B OR C OR A, B, AND C are closed. On some PLC models, branches may be utilized for both inputs and outputs on a rung.

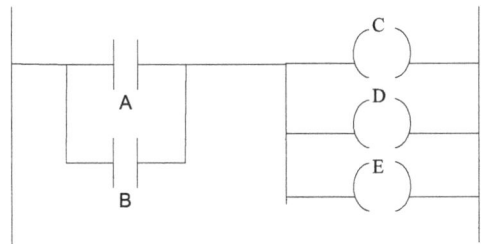

Fig 29.An OR configuration for both inputs and outputs.

Parallel output branching allows a single input to activate multiple outputs simultaneously. Note that if such a configuration is not permitted by the PLC design the ladder diagram may be reconfigured to accommodate the needed functionality. Redesign the ladder using the space below.

MEMORY ORGANIZATION

Memory organization refers to how certain areas of memory in a PLC are utilized. Not all PLC manufacturers organize memory in the same manner but even so the principles involved are the same.

Physical addressing, discussed in a previous section, is the ability to read data from a specific module terminal or write information to a specific module terminal.   When information is read from a contact or input it is stored in memory.   A portion of memory, the input image map, is designated to store this input information.   Each input typically has, at a minimum, a single bit designated to store its information.

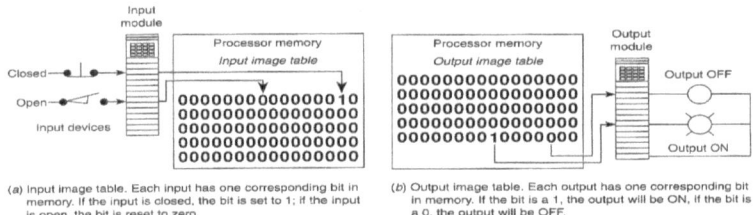

(a) Input image table. Each input has one corresponding bit in memory. If the input is closed, the bit is set to 1; if the input is open, the bit is reset to zero.

(b) Output image table. Each output has one corresponding bit in memory. If the bit is a 1, the output will be ON, if the bit is a 0, the output will be OFF.

Fig 30.Associating input and output data with its corresponding memory location.

Data resulting from logical analysis by the CPU is stored in memory labeled as the output image map.   From this point the information is transferred to a designated output module and then to the particular field device.

This example highlights how portions of memory are designated for particular operations. The memory organization or memory map for a MicroLogix PLC is depicted below.   Each segment is assigned a specific function or assists in the performance of a function.   For instance, the Timer file stores all information related to any timer utilized by the PLC. This includes status, control, and bit information. Timer information will not be stored in the counter file.

Utilizing memory in this manner provides for speedy storage and retrieval of data.   However, the pre-assigned blocks of memory can

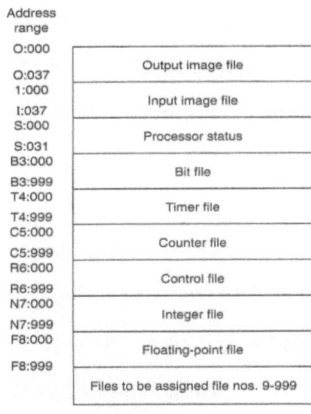

Fig 31.Memory allocation for the MicrolLogix 1000.

lead to inefficiency in cases where all the memory space is allocated but more is needed. There might be free memory in the counter block but this cannot be used since it is designated only for counters.

When referencing timers and counters, each will be identified as T4.0 and C5.0, respectively for the Micrologix 1000. The T4 corresponds to the file location. The 0 identifies the specific timer instance. Each instance has multiple pieces of information associated with it such as timer status and data information.

Memory utilization or assignment in the ControlLogix reflects the schemas incorporated into everyday personal computers. When a timer or counter is added to a ladder diagram the memory addresses are not automatically selected from a predefined block. Most recently designed PLCs will reserve a segment of memory based on the needs of the single device/instruction set. The memory segment is large enough to store all the information related to the device/instruction. For instance, a timer will require memory to store bit status and control bit information so the predefined segment includes locations for each.

This is very similar to the MicroLogix memory schema utilization except the predefined segment can reside anywhere in the RAM of the PLC. The result is memory segments for timers, counters, etc. interspersed throughout the RAM. This produces a much more efficient use of memory but requires more complex storage and retrieval algorithms in comparison to the MicroLogix scheme.

SCANNING PROCESS

The PLC's CPU monitors the status of all inputs. It takes these values and energizes or de-energizes the outputs according to the ladder diagram/user program. This is referred to as scanning. A scan does not consist of a PLC executing ladder diagrams rung by rung. Instead the PLC performs an I/O and program scan. The I/O scan transfers data to and from the output and input modules, respectively. The information is transferred in the form of bits and stored in image tables. Remember image tables are blocks of memory designated to store the input and output bit state. The input and output modules are the portion of the PLC that interface with the outside world. The actual bridge between the physical world and the internal world of the PLC is the optical isolation circuitry.

The scan begins by transferring data from the output image table to the output module. This is followed by the PLC taking a snapshot of the current input signals registered in the input module. This snapshot

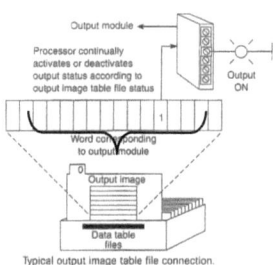

Fig 32.Data flow from the PLC to a controlled output.

48

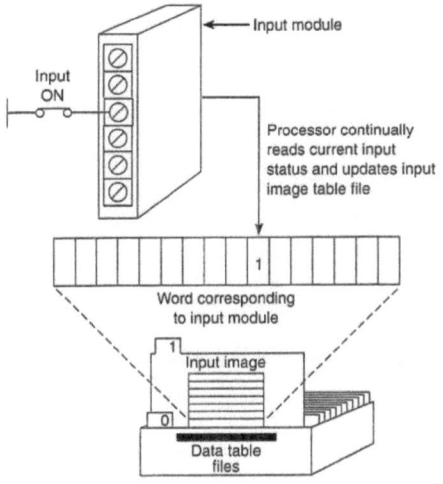

Typical input image table file connection.

Fig 33.Data flow into the PLC from an input source.

of data is transferred from the input module to the input image table. The next phase is the program scan. The CPU utilizes the snapshot of the input image table to perform a logical evaluation via the ladder logic. Results of this logical evaluation are written to the output image map during the final step of the program scan cycle. If a coil is true (active, high) a one is written to the corresponding bit in the output image table, otherwise a zero is written to the bit denoting the contact as false (inactive, low). Therefore, the CPU bases its decisions on states of the inputs prior to entering the program scan. If an input is changed during the scan it will not register until the next scan cycle. Completion of the program scan ends a single scan cycle and then the process begins again with the I/O scan.

<u>Scanning Steps</u>

1. Transfer output map bits to the output module (I/O scan)
2. Input module signals are frozen i.e. snapshot is taken (I/O scan)
3. Transfer input module bits to the input image map (I/O scan)
4. The next phase is initiated by the CPU reading all data bits currently in the input image map (Program scan)
5. CPU evaluates/performs ladder logic on current set of data bits (Program scan)
6. Results of evaluation transferred to the output image map (Program scan)

<u>FAIL-SAFE DESIGN</u>

Fail-Safe Design is the procedure of programming to assure safety of the operator and processes. An example of this type of design is requiring two hand switches and a part presence sensor to be closed before a machine will activate. In this scenario the design ensures there is a part in the machine and both hands of the operator are in a safe location.

Consider the selection of electrical connections from a Fail-Safe standpoint. If wires are cut or connections fail, the equipment should still be safe. For example, if a normally closed stop button is used, and the connector is broken, it will cause the machine to stop as if the stop button has been pressed. Fail-Safe Design rules of thumb for selecting NO or NC devices are as follows:

NO – When wiring switches or sensors that start actions, use normally open switches so if there is a problem with the switch the process will not start.

NC – When wiring switches that stop processes use normally closed switches so if they fail the process will stop.

Fail-Safe also includes scenarios guaranteeing notification of system failure. Housing alarms utilize closed circuits to indicate that a door or window is in the secure position. So if the window or door is opened the circuit is broken and the alarm system registers this as unsecured. Additionally, this method of design ensures that circuit failures will be detected. Wireless alarm systems depend on batteries for each individual door or window. If the battery dies then the failure of the circuit is registered by the alarm system prompting investigation. If an alarm system utilizes open circuits to indicate a secured door or window and closed circuits as unsecured then failure of a circuit may not be detected.

Design of a fail-safe system requires consideration of these all these scenarios.

<u>Timers and Counters</u>

In this module, PLC timer and counter instructions are discussed. After studying this module, the student should be able to:

- List the types of timers and counters used in ladder logic programs;
- Understand how the timers and counters work in ladder logic programs;
- Use status bits of timers and counters to control other instructions;
- Write a ladder logic program using timers and counters.

Three types of timers are used in PLC ladder logic programs. They are ON-delay timers, OFF-delay timers, and retentive timers. Figures show the timer instructions used in the Allen-Bradley PLC.

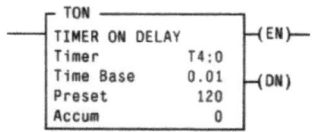

Fig 34.<u>ON-Delay Timer Instruction</u>

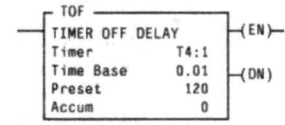

Fig 35.<u>OFF-Delay Timer Instruction</u>

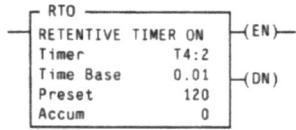

Fig 36.Retentive Timer Instruction

When programming a timer instruction, the programmer must specify the Timer address, the Time Base, and the Preset value, which are listed in the instruction. The format of the Timer address is T4:N, where N is a positive integer. Each timer instruction should have a unique number that distinguishes its timer instruction from other timer instructions. The Time Base value is an interval that the timer is going to use. This value can be set to 1 second, 0.01 second, or 0.001 second. The Preset value specifies how many intervals a timer should count before the timing is complete, also known as "done". A timer's setting time equals its Preset value multiplied by its Time Base. For example, if a timer's Time Base is 0.01 and Preset is 500, the timer's setting time is 500 x 0.01 second = 5 seconds. That means this timer will be done 5 seconds after the timer instruction is enabled.

A timer instruction must be located next to the right rail in a rung. An ON-delay timer is enabled when its rung is true. A rung is true when there is at least one path made by the instructions that are true from the left rail to the timer instruction. An OFF-delay timer is enabled when its rung is false. When a timer is enabled, its Accumulate value shows how many Time Base intervals have elapsed since the timer was activated. A timer is *done* when its Accumulate value reaches its Preset value. When an ON-delay timer or an OFF-delay timer is timing, its rung condition change, i.e. a rung changes from true to false for an

ON-delay timer or a rung changes from false to true for an OFF-delay timer, will cause the timer to stop and its Accumulate value to be reset to zero.

A retentive timer works like an ON-delay timer with one difference. That is, when its rung condition changes from true to false, the timer simply stops timing, but its Accumulate value is not reset to zero. When its rung condition goes from false to true again, the retentive timer's Accumulate value counts up from where it stopped the last time. To reset a retentive timer's Accumulate value to zero, a reset instruction with the same timer address must be used. A reset instruction is a controlled instruction, which means it must be located next to the right rail in a rung. When its rung is true, the reset instruction becomes enabled and resets the timer according to the address that is assigned to the reset instruction.

Each timer instruction has three very useful status bits. These bits are Timer Enable (TE), Timer Timing (TT) and Timer Done (TN). Each of these bits has one bit of memory and the memory is affected by the corresponding bit status.

For an ON-delay timer and a retentive timer

- The Timer Enable bit is high when the timer's rung is true; it is low when the rung is false.
- The Timer Timing bit is high when the timer's rung is true and the Accumulate value is less than the Preset value. This bit is low when the rung is false or after the Accumulate value equals the Preset value.
- The Timer Done bit is high when the rung is true and the timer is done. It is low when the rung is false or before the timer is done.

For an OFF-delay timer

- The Timer Enable bit is high when the timer's rung is false; it is low when the rung is true.
- The Timer Timing bit is high when the timer's rung is false and the Accumulate value is less than the Preset value. This bit is low when the rung is true or after the Accumulate value equals the Preset value.
- The Timer Done bit is high when the rung is false and the timer is done. It is low when the rung is true or before the timer is done.

53

CHAPTER 3: SCADA DESIGN

The SCADA Human Machine Interface (HMI) software provides a graphical representation of the RTU status and alarm history. The SCADA HMI software allows visualization of all process data and operator control over site equipment. Operational and environmental reports can be generated from the SCADA HMI system and summarized data can be stored in historical files of the SCADA HMI system.

SCADA HMI SOFTWARE System Overview, Trends, Alarms, Reports, Historical Data

RSVIEW SCADA HMI SYSTEM FROM ROCKWELL SOFTWARE PROVIDES THE ABILITY TO:

• View facility-wide operationally-centric data

• Capture, store and retrieve critical operational data with operator notes

• View Trend data in real-time from "live" data or historical sources

• Provide high system availability and data integrity

• Preemptive critical alarm notification of operations and maintenance staff via text or voice paging system

• Produce operational and regulatory report on regular intervals.

• Provide system-wide administration of security and log-on rights

COMMUNICATION MEDIA

Lease line modems, radio modems, cellular modems, frame relay, satellite, and microwave are all means of connecting RTUs to a central SCADA HMI system. Rockwell Automation RTUs connect to many Third Party devices to build a complete SCADA system. Rockwell Automation maintains a list of quality communication technology partners in our Encompass Partnering program. We have partnerships with some of the top names in the industry.

INTRODUCTION TO DESIGNING:

Whether describing Oil and Gas or Water Wastewater industries, today's focus on the bottom line and reducing costs put Operators and Engineers under constant pressure to find ways to maximize efficiency.

As an Oil or Gas production or transportation company, you are under constant pressure to maximize production, meet increasingly demanding delivery schedules and reduce operating and maintenance costs while ensuring compliance with environmental regulations and secure operation.

As a Water Wastewater Supervisor, you are expected to ensure public health, protect your local environment, operate your system within

budgetary constraints, and provide secure, uninterruptible wastewater collection and water distribution service to your customers. With increasing government regulations, increasing output and heighten security awareness, many have seen the need to install or upgrade Supervisory Control and Data Acquisition (SCADA) systems. The function of a SCADA system is to monitor, operate and control remote systems that are located over a large geographic area from a central location. Remote monitoring and control can provide data that can be used to significantly enhance operation efficiencies, reduce downtime, and increase security and counterterrorism measures. Other benefits of remote monitoring include better regulatory record keeping and reporting, remote trouble shooting to reduce downtime and increase repair efficiency, reduce time and travel labour cost, and improved capability to instantly alert operators of alarms and undesirable events. Rockwell Automation is a leader in providing high quality, off-the-shelf, hardware and software SCADA solutions for the water and wastewater and Oil & Gas industries. Built with open communication protocols like Ethernet, DF1, and Modbus and support for the most used SCADA protocols like DNP, BSAP and others, our PLC-based Remote Terminal Units (RTUs) offer multiple topology configurations:

• Point to Point

• Point to Multi-point

- Report by Exception
- Broadcast
- Store and Forward

and are supportable by your maintenance staff or local systems integrator using ladder logic programming language. Visualizing and maintaining your system, and informing your operators from a central location is made easy with our RSView SCADA software which comes with I/O drivers to connect to Allen Bradley RTUs as well as most 3rd party RTUs.A SCADA system built with Rockwell Automation hardware and software offers you the best value, scalable solution, that can be expanded and upgraded over time translating into lower longterm risk for your facility.

WASTEWATER TREATMENT

LIFT STATIONS

Collections systems rely on a series of lift stations and combined sewer overflow (CSO) stations communicating to a central location to prevent sewerage back-ups and protect the environment.

WATER BOOSTER STATIONS

Booster pump stations for fresh water systems operate by maintaining system pressure or matching water flow demand.

OIL AND GAS PRODUCTION

OIL AND GAS WELLS

There are two main types of wells: Natural Flow and Artificial Lift wells. Monitoring and remote control requirements depend on the type of well. For natural flow well, surface process variables like flowing /

casing pressure and temperatures and the position of the flowing valve need to be monitored and gas wells include compensated flow calculations. Remote control is limited to the shutdown valve. For artificial lift wells, additional monitoring and control is required to be able to supervise motor or gas lift valves and be able to control those devices.

PUMP STATIONS

Operate by maintaining system pressure or matching flow demand. Multiple pump stations connected to the pipeline and communicating back to a central location are used to deliver crude oil or products to refineries and terminals.

COMPRESSOR

STATIONS

Compressor Stations are responsible in pipeline systems for maintaining the appropriate pressure levels needed to deliver gas at the destination locations. Multiple compressor stations are typically needed in a gas pipeline and the communication to a central location is key to ensure coordination and safety of the operation.

VALVE STATIONS

An important element in the safe operation of a gas or liquid pipeline is the block or segmenting valves. These

valves are mainly responsible for shutting down segments of the pipeline to isolate leaks or ruptures. Local and remote control capabilities as well as data acquisition functions to be able to collect process information along the pipeline (Pressure, temperature, flow and valve position) are the

main requirements of this application.

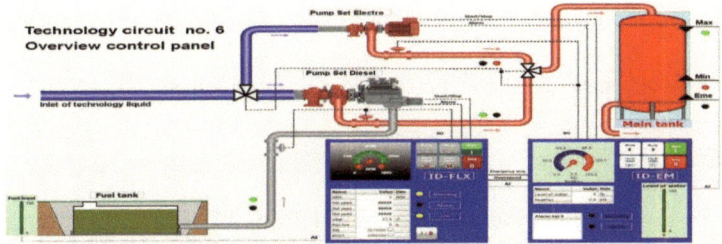

Fig 37.SAMPLE DIAGRAM OF SCADA APPLICATION

CHAPTER 4: ELECTRICAL DRIVES

Introduction: In some countries nearly 65% of the total electric energy produced is consumed by electric motors.

Applications of Electric Drives: Electric Propulsion

- Pumps, fans, compressors

- Plant automation

- Flexible manufacturing systems

- Spindles and servos

- Appliances and power tools

- Cement kilns

- Paper and pulp mills; textile mills

- Automotive applications

- Conveyors, elevators, escalators, lifts.

ELECTRIC DRIVES - A DEFINITION

About 50% of electrical energy produced is used in electric drives today.

Electric drives may run at constant speed or at variable speed.

Energy/Cost Savings

- System efficiency can be increased from 15% to 27% by introducing variable-speed drive operation in place of constant-speed operation.

- For a large pump variable-speed drive, payback period ~ 3-5 years whereas operating life is ~ 20 years.

Electric Machines -An engineer designing a high-performance drive system must have intimate knowledge about machine performance and Power Electronics.

- DC Machines - shunt, series, compound, separately excited dc motors and switched reluctance machines.

- AC Machines - Induction, wound rotor synchronous, permanent magnet synchronous, synchronous reluctance, and switched reluctance machines.

- Special Machines - switched reluctance machines.

All of the above machines are commercially available in fractional kW to MW ranges except permanent-magnet, synchronous, synchronous reluctance, and switched reluctance which are available up to 150 kW level.

Selection Criteria for Electric Machines

- Cost

- Thermal Capacity

- Efficiency

- Torque-speed profile

- Acceleration

- Power density, volume of motor

- Ripple, cogging torques

- Peak torque capability

Electrical Drives

- About 50% of electrical energy used for drives

- Can be either used for fixed speed or variable speed 75% - constant speed, 25% variable speed (expanding).

Example on VSD application

Constant speed

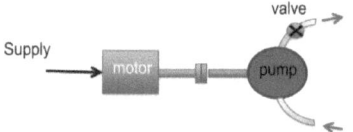

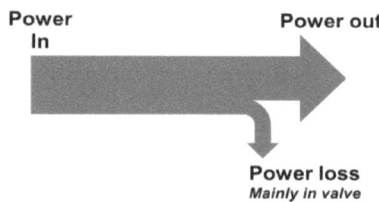

Fig 38.VSD Application

Variable Speed Drives

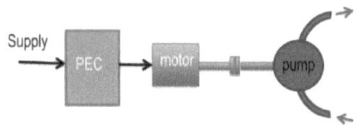

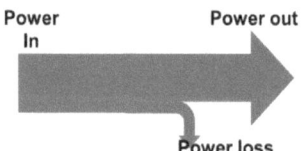

Fig 39.Conventional electric drives (variable speed)

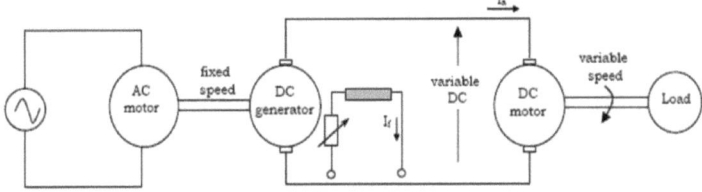

- Bulky
- Inefficient
- inflexible

Fig 40.Modern electric drives (With power electronic converters)

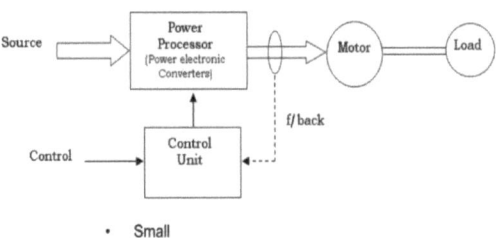

- Small
- Efficient
- Flexible

Fig 41.Modern electric drives

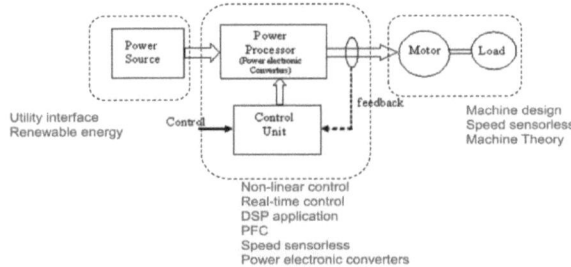

- Inter-disciplinary
- Several research area
- Expanding

Fig 42.Controllers

Controllers embody the control laws governing the load and motor characteristics and their interaction.

Fig 43.Controllers Components

Components in electric drives

Motors

- DC motors - permanent magnet – wound field

- AC motors – induction, synchronous , brushless DC

- Applications, cost, environment

Power sources

- DC – batteries, fuel cell, photovoltaic - unregulated

- AC – Single- three- phase utility, wind generator - unregulated

Power processor

- To provide a regulated power supply

- Combination of power electronic converters

- More efficient

- Flexible

- Compact

- AC-DC   DC-DC DC-AC   AC-AC

Control unit

- Complexity depends on performance requirement

- analog- noisy, inflexible, ideally has infinite bandwidth.

- digital – immune to noise, configurable, bandwidth is smaller than the analog controller's

- DSP/microprocessor – flexible, lower bandwidth - DSPs perform faster operation than microprocessors (multiplication in single cycle), can perform complex estimations.

DC Motors

- Advantage: simple torque and speed control without sophisticated electronics

- Limitations:

- Regular Maintenance

- Heavy motor

- Expensive motor

- Sparking

DC DRIVES Vs AC DRIVES

DC drives:

Advantage in control unit

Disadvantage in motor

AC Drives:

Advantage in motor

Disadvantage in control unit

Load

The motor drives a load that has a characteristic torque vs. speed requirement.

In general, load torque is a function of speed and can be written as:

$$T_l \propto \omega_m^x$$

x=1 for frictional systems (e.g. feed drives)

x=2 for fans and pumps.

General Torque Equation

Translational (linear) motion:

$$F = M \frac{dv}{dt}$$

F : Force (Nm)
M : Mass (Kg)
v : velocity (m/s)

Rotational motion:

$$T = J \frac{d\omega}{dt}$$

T : Torque (Nm)
J : Moment of Inertia (Kgm²)
ω : angular velocity (rad/s)

Torque Equation: Motor drives

$$T_e = T_L + J \frac{d\omega}{dt} \quad or \quad T_e - T_L = J \frac{d\omega}{dt}$$

Te : motor torque (Nm) T_L : Load torque (Nm)

$$T_e - T_L > 0 \quad \text{Acceleration}$$

$$T_e - T_L < 0 \quad \text{Deceleration}$$

$$T_e - T_L = 0 \quad \text{Constant speed}$$

Drive accelerates or decelerates depending on whether Te is greater or less than T_L During acceleration, motor must supply not only the load torque but also dynamic torque, (Jdw/dt).

During deceleration, the dynamic torque, (Jdw/dt), has a negative sign. Therefore, it assists the motor torque, Te.

Elementary principles of mechanics

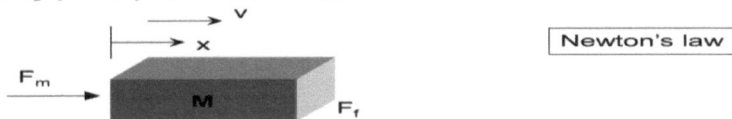

Newton's law

Linear motion, constant M

- First order differential equation for speed
- Second order differential equation for displacement

Fig 44. Newton's law for linear motion

Elementary principles of mechanics

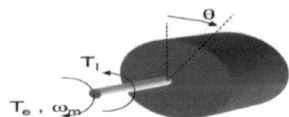

Rotational motion

- Normally is the case for electrical drives

$$T_e - T_l = \frac{d(J\omega_m)}{dt}$$

With constant J,

- First order differential equation for angular frequency (or velocity)
- Second order differential equation for angle (or position)

Fig 45. Rotational motion with constant J

Elementary principles of mechanics

For constant J,

$$T_e = T_l + J\frac{d\omega_m}{dt}$$

$J\dfrac{d(\omega_m)}{dt}$ Torque dynamic – present during speed transient

$\dfrac{d(\omega_m)}{dt}$ Angular acceleration (speed)

The larger the net torque, the faster the acceleration is.

CHAPTER 5: APPLICATIONS OF PLC IN INDUSTRY

1. Controlling the Filling and Capping Operation of a Bottling Plant using PLC and SCADA

At first a set of empty bottle is run by using a conveyer towards filling section, after the operation, the filled bottles are sent towards the capping section. After successful capping operation, the sealed bottles terminate towards exit and a new set of empty bottle arrive, in this way the process continues. This paper includes the method using which, a bunch of bottles can be filled and capped at one instant of time. This method has made the operation more flexible and time saving.

The filling and capping operations are controlled using Programmable Logic Controllers (PLC), as the PLC's are very much user-efficient, cost-effective and easy to control. By using PLC automation the whole process is kept under control. SCADA (Supervisory Control and Data Acquisition) is used to monitor the process by means of a display system.

Industrial Automation is the use of Control Systems to control Industrial Machinery and Processes, reducing the need for human intervention.

If we compare a job being done by human and by Automation, the physical part of the job is replaced by use of a Machine, whereas the mental capabilities of the human are replaced with the Automation.

The human sensory organs are replaced with electrical, mechanical or electronic Sensors to enable the Automation systems to perform the job.

Higher level of human intelligence like planning, analysis, prediction and intuitive decision making is not done by this Level of Automation.

Automation plays very important role in today's world economy. One of the most important applications of automation process is in beverages and soft drinks industries, where continuous filling and capping process is carried out. If human effort or mechanical effort is used in this field then it is very much tough to perform this long and continuous process and so it is being substituted by automation process which completes the task with very much ease.

As mentioned above, our paper is also an application where the automation process is used to control the filling and capping operation in a bottling plant to reduce the human effort using Programmable Logic Controllers and SCADA (Supervisory Control and Data Acquisition).

To develop the programming to control a bottling plant by using PLC Automation we must first develop the ladder logic, after that the programming part can be developed.

After successful completion of the programming part, we have to animate the HUMAN- MACHINE INTERFACE or the HMI or SCADA.

CONSTRUCTION:

The basic construction of the aforesaid processes of a bottling plant i.e. filling and capping is consisted of various steps. At first a conveyer belt is installed which will run the set of bottle through different stages. After that, in the filling section the necessary arrangements are done so that the filling process can take place by means of some filling pipes, containing the beverage or soft drink. In case of capping section also, some arrangements are done so that the capping process can be done without any error. To implement this steps , sensors are used so that in filling section, the pipes can sense the presence of the bottles and they can be filled. In capping section also, the sensors are used to cap the set of bottle with ease. The filling process is based on the preset value of a counter, depending upon which the pump is switched on for that particular period of time.

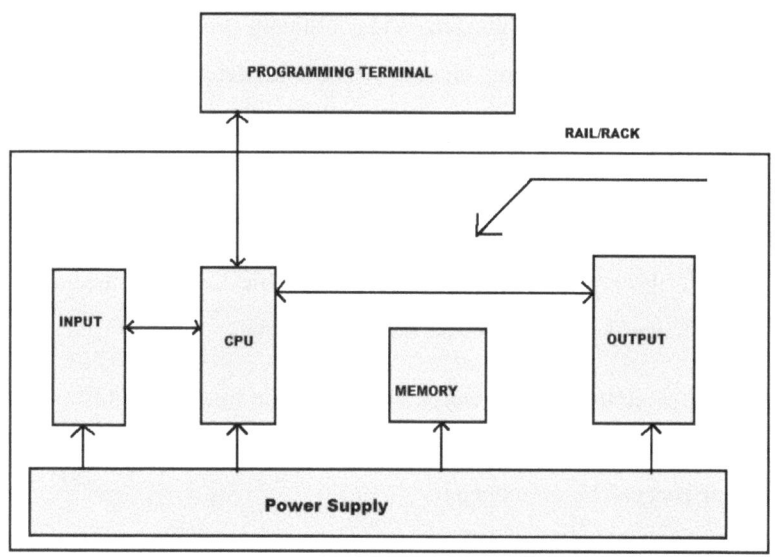

Fig 46.BLOCK DIAGRAM OF A PLC

PROCESS DESCRIPTION AND CASE STUDY IN FACTORY

In our paper we have specialised on ROCKWELL PLC, in which the RSLOGIX 5000 software is the main platform to control the basic operations. The ladder logic, i.e. the programming part is done with the help of the above mentioned software. After successful completion of the programming, it is transferred to a virtual emulator which is already installed on the same workstation. As in case of a bottling plant, huge manpower is needed and as it is also very costly to implement the plant, we have given the basic priority to its security. The virtual emulator gives us the output whether the programming is correct or not. After the programming is made error free, it is installed on the main plc in the bottling plant.

Using plc programming the process of capping and filling is done simultaneously and as it is controlled by automation there is no need of constant manpower to handle the plant. There is one control room where the SCADA output is constantly observed by a person from where he can keep his close eye on various stages of the plant by using SCADA display. In case of emergency, the whole plant can be controlled from that control room only.

In this paragraph of our paper a detailed explanation of the various basic operations of a bottling plant is given. The filling and capping processes take place simultaneously.

At first an empty set of bottles are placed on a conveyer belt. When the conveyer is started, the empty set of bottles start moving towards the filling section. After reaching the filling section the conveyer is stopped and the filling pipes then start filling the empty bottles. When the bottle filling is done then the conveyer again gets motion and the filled set of bottles move towards capping section. The set of bottles when reach the capping section again the conveyer gets stop and then capping process takes place. Completion of the capping process brings the conveyer again into motion and the set of filled and capped bottles move towards exit for further modification. This is a simultaneous process which is totally handled by PLC programming and in this way continuous filling and capping process takes place in a bottling plant.

Fig 47.COCA-COLA BOTTLING PLANT

CONTROL PHILOSOPHY:

1. In a bottling plant there are two sections in it, Filling and Capping.

2. For the operation of the plant there will be 3 push-buttons.

3. The push-buttons will represent START, STOP, PAUSE.

4. The proximity sensor will sense the finished bottles as it passes by it in the conveyer belt.

5. The START button will start the whole system and also reset the counter to zero.

6. The STOP button will stop the whole system but it won't reset the counter value to zero, the numeric display will show the last counted value.

7. The RESET-COUNTER will reset the counter to zero.

8. If the PAUSE button is pressed then the system will hold its position and stop, and when it is pressed again the system will resume.

SCADA DESIGN

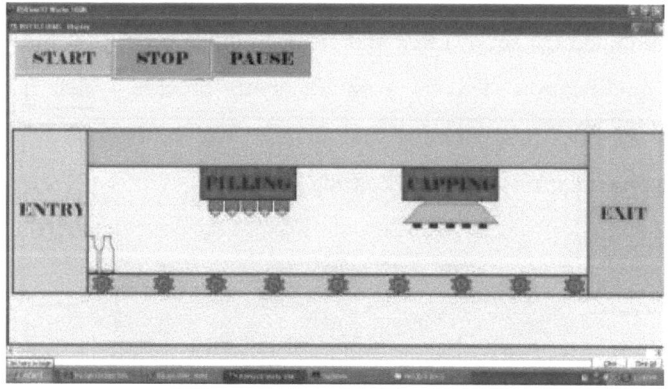

Fig 48: CONVEYER ON

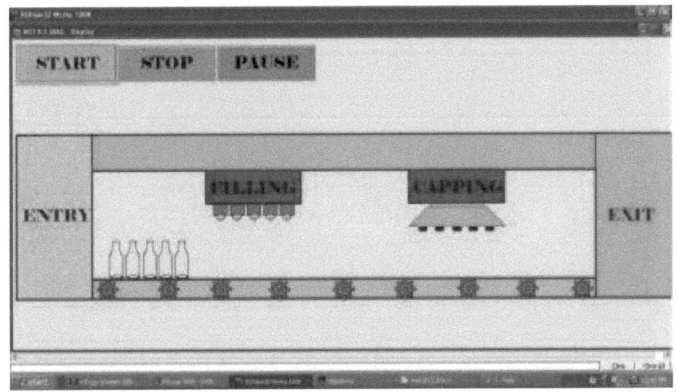

Fig 49: EMPTY BOTTLES RUNNING

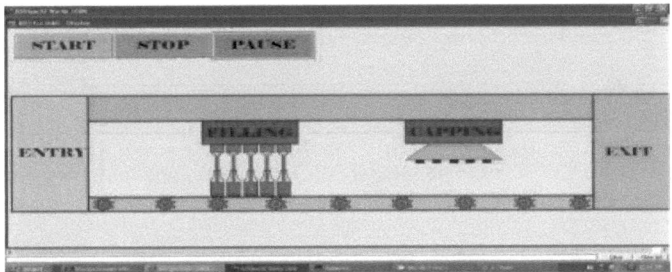

Fig 50:BOTTLES FILLING

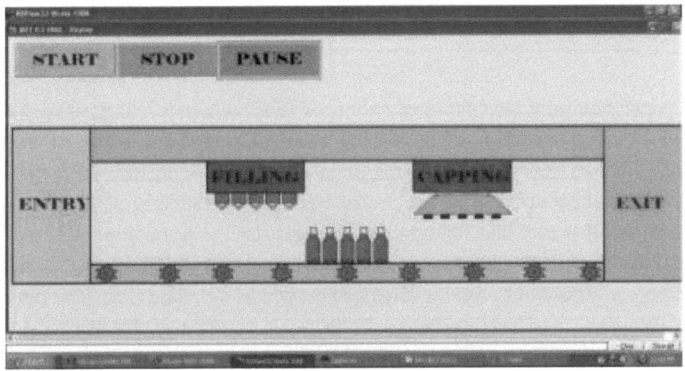

Fig 51:FILLED BOTTLES RUNNING

71

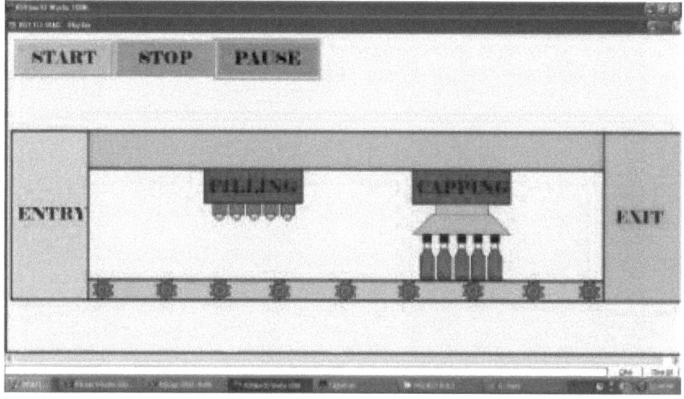

Fig 52: CAPPING SECTION

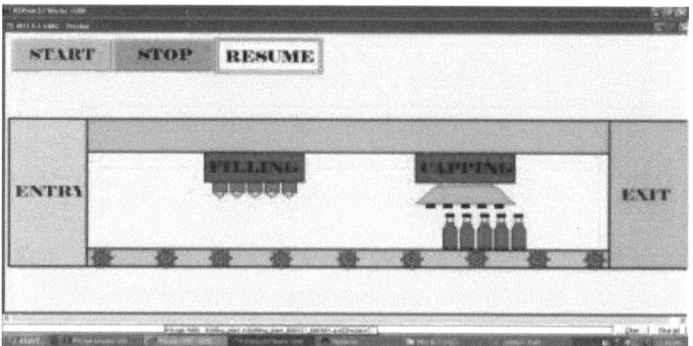

Fig 53:SET OF BOTTLES RUNNING TOWARDS EXIT

This paper has suggested the application of fully automated untouched plc controlled filling and capping operation of a bottling plant. The system works in high speed of production with very much accuracy and precision. This system meets the market demand with a few mechanical effort. The system has been proved working without wastage or spill out of the liquid. It is true that for small scale industries the installation cost of PLC is very much high but it has many advantages which overcomes the instllation cost. In this paper it is suggested how a set of bottle can be filled and capped at the same time. The other additional feature of this paper, here it is explained the SCADA design also. By using the SCADA the whole process can be monitored from a single control room only and necessary steps can be taken in case of emergency.

APPLICATIONS OF PLC IN INDUSTRY

2. Pump Control Process Via Star Delta Starter Using Programmable Logic Controller And SCADA

This paper presents the starting operation of a pump using star delta starter. In a pumping system the basic need is to start it and to control its level. Star delta starter helps to start the pump and the level sensors help to control the water level in the tank. At first the pump system is kept in offline mode and the low level sensor shows the level of the water in the tank. The SCADA display shows it with a red light on the display board. When the start button is pressed, the motor seeks permission from the low level sensor and after that the motor starts with the help of MAIN and STAR contact of the star delta starter. When the system is ON the SCADA display shows green light on the board which further indicates that the MAIN contact of the starter is closed.

The entire process is controlled by programmable logic controllers, as they are very much reliable, effective and cost-efficient. The SCADA display shows the entire system in a display board, which helps the system to be monitored in real time.

Industrial Automation is the use of Control Systems to control Industrial Machinery and Processes, reducing the need for human intervention. If we compare a job being done by human and by Automation, the physical part of the job is replaced by use of a Machine, whereas the mental capabilities of the human are replaced with the Automation.

The human sensory organs are replaced with electrical, mechanical or electronic Sensors to enable the Automation systems to perform the job.

Higher level of human intelligence like planning, analysis, prediction and intuitive decision making is not done by this Level of Automation.

Automation plays very important role in today's world economy. Water is the most needed resource in whole world and thus the storage of water is also a very important task to be carried out. A pumping system is needed to store water in tank.

One of the most used fields of automation is in pump control system. The pump control system can be started and controlled by using automation technology. Water level in the tank can be monitored using sensors and the pump can be started using star delta starter.

To develop the programming to control a pump system using automation technology, we must first develop the ladder logic, after that the programming part can be done. The monitoring unit can be developed using SCADA (Supervisory Control And Data Acquisition).

Construction of a pump system consists of several parts. The most important parts of a pumping system is a reservoir, a motor and a tank. Other auxiliary elements like pipes, pipe joints, inlet valve, pump stand, tank stands are also needed to construct a pumping system perfectly. Some sensors are also needed to monitor the water level inside the tank.

At first, the reservoir, the pump and the tank is joined by means of pipes and pipe joints. An inlet valve is placed between the pump and the reservoir. The pump and the tank is safely mounted on respective stands. Two sensors viz. Low level sensor and high level sensors is installed inside the tank such that they we can monitor the water level inside the tank. When the low level sensor monitors that the water level is low inside the tank it automatically shows that in the SCADA display board with the help of a red light. The pump then automatically starts with the help of star delta starter. The MAIN and the STAR connection comes into direct contact and the pump starting process takes place. The inlet valve thus opens up and the water starts flowing from the reservoir towards the tank. This process continues until and unless the high level sensors senses the water level of the tank, and when it senses that the tank is full it displays the instruction in the SCADA display board with a green light, and the pump automatically stops and so the supply from the reservoir.

STAR DELTA STARTER

Power Circuit:- This is very common type of starter and extensively used, compared to the other types of the starters. A star-delta starter is used for a cage motor designed to run normally on delta connected starter winding. When the switch is in the START position, the stator winding is connected in star. When the motor picks up speed, say 80 percent of its rated value, the star contact is disconnected and the delta contact is ON. By connecting the stator winding, first in star then in delta the line current drawn by motor at starting is reduced at the time of starting when the stator winding are star connected, each stator phase gets a voltage $V_L/1.732$, where V_L is the line voltage since the torque developed by an induction motor is proportional to the square of the voltage. Star-delta starter reduce the starting torque to one third of that obtained by direct delta starting.

Control Circuit:- After pressing the start push button the on-delay timer, the (KIT), the MAIN contractor (KM3) & the STAR contractor (KM1) gets on. Since there is a feedback of the MAIN contractor with the START push button, so even after releasing the START

74

push button the control circuit remains on. After a predefined time, when the ON-DELAY timer starts giving output , the STAR contractor gets open since according to the control circuit when the delay will be over then the NO attached to the STAR contractor will get open. Since a NO of timer output is connected to the DELTA contractor (KM2) so now the DELTA contactor will get closed. Two interlocking KM1 & KM2 are used as N.C (Normally Closed) in STAR and DELTA network respectively. This process is done to prevent the starting of STAR & DELTA contact at the same time. After pressing the stop push button or when there is overload in the system then the whole system will turn off.

CONTROL PHILOSOPHY:

1. Preconditions to start the system.

Tank level low (Measured by low level digital sensor)

 Inlet pressure is high (Measured by PL digital pressure sensor.

Motor over load healthy

2. How to start the motor

After pressing the Start push button, the pump starts through Star-delta starter.

When the tank level is high, pump will automatically turn off.

3. How to stop the motor

After pressing the Stop push button system will turn off.

4. Safety conditions to run the system:

Motor over load healthy

Inlet valve open and inlet pressure high.

LADDER LOGIC:

Ladder logic or ladder diagrams are the most common programming language used to program a PLC. Ladder logic was one of the first programming approaches used in PLC's. The symbols used in relay ladder logic consist of a power rail to the left, second power rail to the right. The logic of each circuit or rung is also from left to right. A common mistake is made that is trying to think of the diagram as the current across the rung for output to function. There are many logic symbols are used in ladder logic like counters, timers, math, data etc.

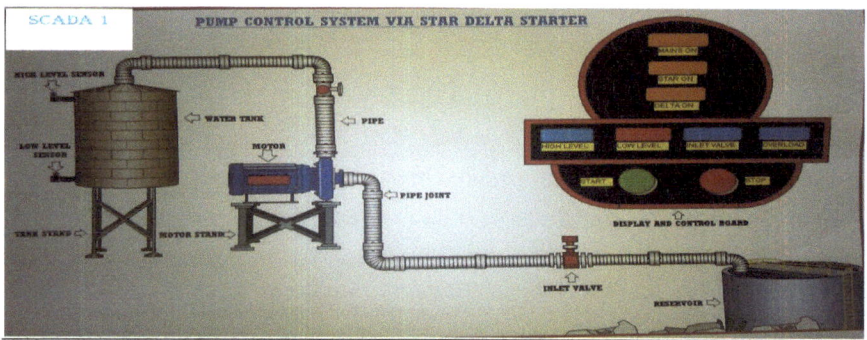

Fig 54: Pump Control System Via Star-delta Starter

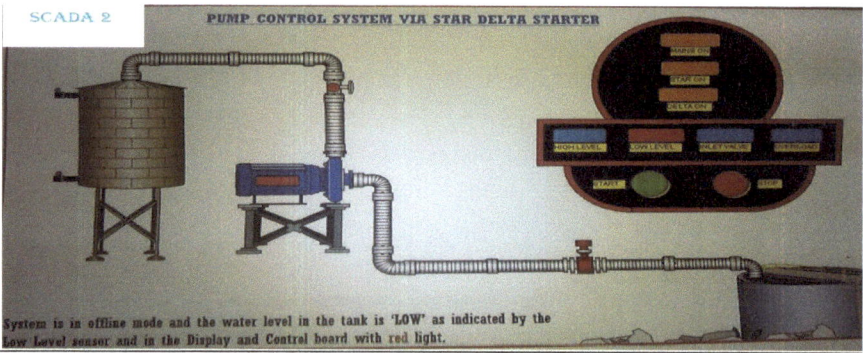

Fig 55: System is offline

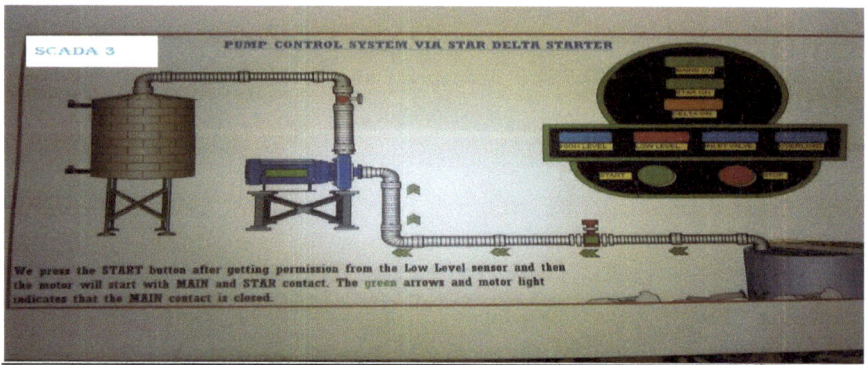

Fig56. Motor starts

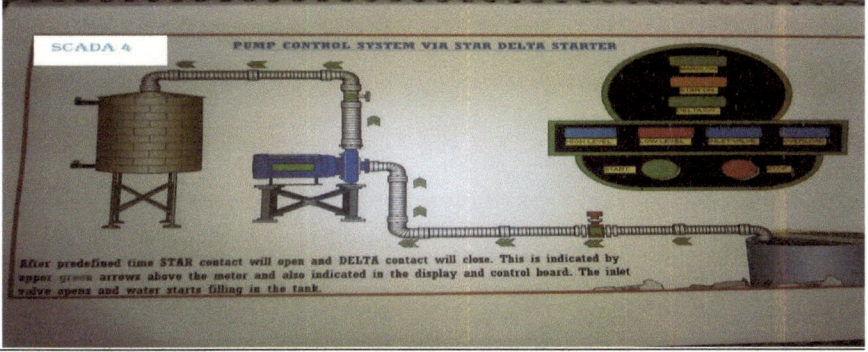

Fig57. Water starts filling the tank

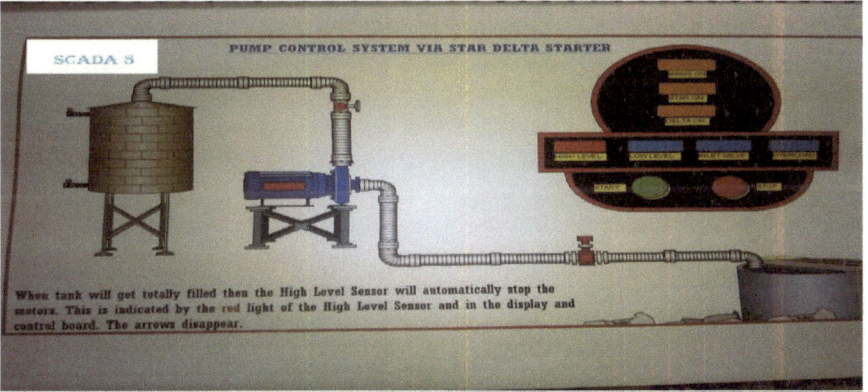

Fig58. Motor stops when the level is high.

Chapter 6: Future Aspects

As discussed in the book, one can easily conclude that in near future, there going to be a huge application of PLCs and SCADA designs in industries, as it reduces the human effort, makes the task more precise and reliable. Our book has mentioned some of the applications of the PLCs but there are huge number of applications are readily available to be implemented. If today's industry can accept the applications of PLCs there will be huge change in the industry applications.

References:

[1] Shaukat.N, ,PLC based automatic liquid filling process, Multi Topic Conference 2002,IEEE publications.

[2] Dunning Gray (1998) - 'Introduction to Programmable Logic Controllers' - Delmar publishers, pp.421-428.

[3] Petruzella, Frank D. (2010) - 'Programmable logic Controllers' - Tata McGraw Hill Education, pp.6-12.

[4] Ahmed Ullah Abu Saeed, Md. Al-Mamun and A. H. M. Zadidul Karim, "Industrial Application of PLCs in Bangladesh,"International Journal of Scientific & Engineering Research, vol.3, Issue 6, June 2012.

[5] Stuart A. Boyer, Scada – Supervisory Control and Data Acquisition, International Society of Automation USA, 4th Edison, 2009.

[6] Mallaradhya H. M., K. R. Prakash, "Automatic Liquid Filling to Bottles of Different Height Using Programmable Logic Controller," in proceedings of AECE-IRAJ International Conference, July 2013, pp. 122-124.

[7] T. Kalaiselvi, R. Praveena, Aakanksha R. and Dhanya S., "PLC Based Automatic Bottle Filling and Capping System with User Defined Volume Selection," International Journal of Emerging Technology and Advanced Engineering, vol. 2, Issue 8, August 2012, pp. 134-137.

[8] Shaukat N., "PLC Based Automatic Liquid Filling Process,"IEEE Multi Topic Conference, 2002.

[9] http://www.industry.siemens.com/verticals/global/en/food-beverage/beverage industry/Documents/E20001-A100-T110-V1-7600.pdf

[10] Ashwini P. Somavanshi, Supriya B. Asutkar and Sachin A.More, "Automatic Bottle Filling Using Microcontroller Volume Correction," International Journal of Engineering Research and Technology IJERT, vol. 2, Issue 3, March 2013, pp. 1-4.

[11]COCA COLA BOTTLING PLANT; http://www.profibus.com/technology/profibus/case-studies/coca-cola-bottling-plant-at-hm-interdrink-germany/

[12]www.rockwellautomation.com

[13] basic plc.ppt

[14] Introduction to Programmable Logic Controllers

[15] 2-ladders